Be My Guest

Be My Guest

Sermons on the Lord's Supper

C. Thomas Hilton

PROTESTANT PULPIT EXCHANGE

Abingdon Press
Nashville

BE MY GUEST: SERMONS ON THE LORD'S SUPPER

Hilton, C. Thomas (Clifford Thomas)
    Be my guest : sermons on the Lord's Supper / C. Thomas Hilton.
        p.   cm.– (The Protestant pulpit exchange)
    Includes bibliographical references.
    ISBN 0-687-02822-1 (alk. paper)
        1. Communion sermons.   2. Sermons, American.   3. Presbyterian Church–Sermons.   I. Title.   II. Series.
        BV4257.5.H55   1991
        234' . 163–dc20   91-7713
                                                                             CIP

Scripture quotations, unless otherwise indicated, are from the New Revised Standard Version Bible, copyright © 1989, by the Division of Christian Education of the National Council of the Churches of Christ in the United States of America.

Scripture quotations noted GNB are from the *Good News Bible*–Old Testament: Copyright © American Bible Society 1976; New Testament: Copyright © American Bible Society 1966, 1971, 1976. Used by permission.

Scripture quotations noted REB are from *The Revised English Bible.* Copyright © 1989 by The Delegates of the Oxford University Press and The Syndics of the Cambridge University Press. Reprinted by permission.

Scripture quotations noted KJV are from the King James Version of the Bible.

The excerpt from "The Wonder of It All," by George Beverly Shea, on p. 31, copyright © 1957 by Chancel Music, Inc. Assigned to The Rodeheaver Co. © Renewed 1985 by The Rodeheaver Co. (a division of Word, Inc.). All rights reserved. International copyright secured. Used by permission.

MANUFACTURED IN THE UNITED STATES OF AMERICA

To Jan

Contents

Introduction

Preaching Holy Communion

The Lord's Supper is first and foremost the Lord's. It seems obvious, but the implications are not so obvious. Because it is his supper, he is the host. He invites us. He hovers over the event. He is sad when we do not accept his invitation. He promises his presence. He draws up the agenda for our time together. He is in charge of the timing. He will see to it that it is a significant event. He initiated it in the upper room when he called upon us to continue doing it "in remembrance of me."

How often should we do it? John Calvin said every Sunday. The Roman Catholics do it every day. Some do it quarterly. Where should we do it? Some say only in the chancel, with a priest officiating. Others claim it is a "movable feast" and may be observed anywhere with anyone officiating. When should we do it? It is appropriate only in worship, say some. Others have been most moved by its celebration out in the woods at a youth retreat. In what manner should it be done? Some will come forward to receive it standing before a minister, while others will remain in the pew as elders serve them, while still others will come forward and kneel at the altar railing.

The church seems to be saying that on all but one of these issues we will be flexible. The one issue we will not bend is the one of ownership. The observance is the Lord's. It is the Lord's Supper.

This observance is a sacrament. A sacrament, at its very least, is a sign or symbol of a spiritual reality. We are used to all kinds of symbols denoting ethereal realities. A rectangular piece of cloth painted with white stars and red and white stripes should not be desecrated, because it is a symbol of an ethereal reality—our country. An octagonal piece of metal, painted red with four white letters spelling *stop* symbolizes the ethereal authority of the state. When we do not obey it, we can get into trouble. A friendly wave of the hand is a symbol of an ethereal reality of friendship. Flowers given on an anniversary symbolize the ethereal reality of affection. The bread and wine of the Lord's Supper are but two of many symbols denoting ethereal realities in our life. The difference is in the substance of the Reality.

This is a sacrament of the church. It is not the minister's sacrament, or the layperson's sacrament, for it has been given to the church by the head of the church for the spiritual nourishment of all his people. It is available to members of the church (for some, only confirmed members; for others, baptized members also). It is meant for all who believe in Jesus Christ as their Lord and Savior. It is meant to spiritually strengthen the church so that we might be empowered by the Spirit of God.

The following Communion sermons have all been preached from particular pulpits in local churches just prior to celebrating the sacrament. The observances were organized around the Advent season, New Year's Eve, Lenten season, World Communion, and other occasions. Their relative brevity was mandated by the parameters of an hour-long service. The final chapter includes illustrations from other Communion sermons not included in this book.

"Words, words, words," said Eliza Doolittle in *My Fair Lady,* "I'm so sick of words." Words can be tiresome. Jesus' actions spoke louder than words on the cross and in the Lord's Supper. There are about four thousand dialects in the world, and the words used to communicate meaning are often misunderstood. Body language is usually more explicit. "This is my body that is for you. Do this in remembrance of me" (I Cor. 11:24). I hope you will see Jesus Christ in his body language on the cross, in the Lord's Supper, and in these sermons.

C. Thomas Hilton
First Presbyterian Church
Pompano Beach, Florida

ADVENT COMMUNION 1

> *Return to your stronghold, O prisoners of hope;*
> *today I declare that I will restore to you double.*
> *(Zech. 9:12)*

Prisoners of Hope

This is a time of longing. It is a time of expectation. Advent hymns express the mood well:

> Come, thou long expected Jesus,
> Born to set thy people free;
> From our fears and sins release us,
> Let us find our rest in thee.

Come, come, come.

One Advent hymn has a dialogue going on between the watchman and the traveler:

> Watchman, tell us of the night,
> What its signs of promise are.
> Traveler, o'er yon mountain's height
> See that glory-beaming star!
> Watchman, does its beauteous ray
> Aught of joy or hope foretell?
> Traveler, yes, it brings the day,
> promised day of Israel.

They were watching and waiting and asking each other what the signs of the times meant. They were hoping against hope that it might be the "promised day of Israel."

Another Advent hymn is a plea that Emmanuel (which in English means "God with us") should come soon:

O come, O come, Emmanuel,
and ransom captive Israel,
that mourns in lonely exile here
until the Son of God appear.

. . . Disperse the gloomy clouds of night,
And death's dark shadows put to flight. . . .
. . . Bid envy, strife and discord cease;
fill the whole world with heaven's peace.

The people of the Old Testament were aching for the coming
of the Savior, for Emmanuel, God with us. They wanted things
to change. They wanted a new beginning. They were ready for
a conversion experience, so that they could go in a different
direction. They knew that something was wrong with their
world and, in particular, with their lives. They felt as if they
were captives, and so they called out to Emmanuel to come
and "ransom captive Israel," to come and set them free.

They felt like prisoners. They wanted out, but they could
not get out. They wanted a better life, but they could not find
a better life. They knew that life was meant to be more than it
was for them. Somehow they felt that life was meant to be
abundant, but they couldn't seem to find the door to enter
into that abundant living. They felt cornered, limited, cap-
tured, imprisoned. Zechariah, in our text, picked up on that
frustrated feeling of wanting to be more than he was, but he
did not know how to change his present existence, and he
referred to the Israelites as "prisoners."

> "*Prisoners of our possessions, captives of our
> culture, handcuffed by our habits.*"

North Americans know what it is to be "prisoners." Oh, I
don't mean that we have literally been inside a prison,
behind barbed wire and high walls, with metal bars on the

windows. I mean that we have often, even Christians in the church, found ourselves prisoners of our possessions, captives of our culture, and handcuffed by our habits. We have been "in the world," and "of the world." You doubt this? Play this little mind game with me.

Ask yourself what it is you fear the most. What do you worry about the most often? Around what issues do you lose the most sleep? Are the answers to these questions all related to material possessions? Or are you lying awake at night, worrying about the homeless and starving? Many affluent Christians are prisoners of their abundance. They can't live without it. They can't stop acquiring it. They define themselves as people who have many things, and they can't share them with others, for to share in any significant way means that they would have less with which to define who they are. They are caught; they are captive; they are prisoners of their things. They are compulsive buyers and spenders and acquirers and getters. They are not giving people; they are consumers. Ever shopped at a discount store? "Attention K-Mart shoppers, the blue light special. . . ." That's all they think we are—shoppers who are excited about "blue light specials," prisoners who can't escape. You don't have to be in jail to be a prisoner. All you have to be is controlled by something or someone else. You are not in control of your life. When Zechariah called the religious people of his day "prisoners," they knew, and we know, what he meant.

But it wasn't all bad. They were "prisoners of hope." They were locked into hoping, to yearning, to desiring, to pleading. They were people who daydreamed about a new way of life. They dared to hope.

The theologian Emil Brunner has written in his book *Eternal Hope:* "Hope is the positive . . . mode of awaiting the future. . . . What oxygen is for the lungs, such is hope for the meaning of human life. Take oxygen away and death occurs through suffocation, take hope away and humanity is constricted through lack of breath. . . . No work of (humankind) . . . can be successfully performed without hope."

The psalms remind us of how the Israelites had only hope. They had to wait for a better future, as they yearned for a better life:

Truly the eye of the LORD is on . . .
   those who hope in his steadfast love,
to deliver their souls from death,
   and to keep them alive in famine . . . .
Let your steadfast love, O Lord, be upon us,
   even as we hope in you. (Ps. 33:18-19, 22)

All they had was hope, a yearning for a better future.

> ## *"To be locked into hope is fine, but it is not enough."*

Again, the psalmist asked:

Why are you cast down, O my soul,
   and why are you disquieted within me?
Hope in God; for I shall again praise him,
   my help and my God. (43:5)

So the bad news/good news is that they were "prisoners," but "prisoners of hope." Well, actually that is only bad news, for that is not enough in this life. To be locked into hope is fine, but it is not enough. To be looking for a better tomorrow is admirable, but that is not enough. When you know that you have been created for greater things, it is not enough to live for lesser things.

I suppose it was enough then, for it was all they had before the first Christmas. But Paul, when he wrote to the church in Corinth, caught the biblical vision, for he said that if we have only hope, we are "of all people most to be pitied" (I Cor.

15:19). Hope is fine, but it is not enough after Jesus Christ has come, for our hope has now become a reality.

This is why we have arrived at his holy table as we begin the Advent season. He fulfills our most ambitious hopes. He sets the prisoners free. Jesus Christ exemplifies our most optimistic religious dreams. He is the hope of the world. God sets the prisoners free by visiting our earth in Jesus Christ, and through his death and resurrection he fulfills our deepest hopes.

ADVENT COMMUNION 2

---

*But when the right time finally came, God
sent his own Son. (Gal. 4:4 GNB)*

Plenty of Time

I keep thinking that I should be finished with my Christmas shopping by now. After all, it was six weeks ago that I saw my first Christmas decorations at the mall. Certainly Christmas must be just around the corner. I had better get going. I had better hurry. I had better hustle. Time is fleeting. Pretty soon it will be too late. Hurry, hurry, hurry!

But wait a minute. Today is only the first Sunday of Advent. Christmas Sunday is four weeks from today. I have plenty of time to prepare. That's why the church has an Advent season. The word *advent* is a conjunction of two Latin words that together mean "to come toward." The next four weeks are a time to prepare for the celebration of God's visit to our small planet in the form of a baby in Bethlehem.

I'm not really concerned about your Christmas gift or Christmas cards or house decorating or plane tickets or all of the other aspects of the secular celebration. The secular celebration of Christmas is a lot of fun, but it has very little to do with Christ's birth. You may not have enough time to prepare for Christmas if your celebration is simply secular. But for your spiritual celebration of Christmas, you have plenty of time. Take a deep breath. Relax!

Michel Quoist is a French priest who has written a contemporary prayer on the use of time. Listen to a portion of it, for it prepares us to use our time for spiritual purposes:

Lord, I have time. I have plenty of time. All the time that you give me. The years of my life, the days of my years, the hours of my days, they are all mine. Mine to fill, quietly, calmly, but to fill completely, up to the brim, to offer them to you. . . .

I am not asking you . . . Lord, for time to do this and then that, but your grace to do conscientiously, in that time that you give me, what you want me to do. (Michel Quoist, *Prayers* [New York: Sheed and Ward, 1963])

The Gospel of Mark gives us a good hint of the kind of mood that we ought to have as people of faith during this holy season. Jesus said, "Therefore, keep awake—for you do not know when the master of the house will come, in the evening, or at midnight, or at cockcrow, or at dawn, or else he may find you asleep when he comes suddenly. And what I say to you I say to all: Keep awake" (Mark 13:35-37).

Other versions of this passage have Jesus telling us to "keep on the alert," to "stay awake," and to "watch for [his] return." While it is true that some Christians are so concerned about Jesus' second coming that they forget to celebrate his first coming at Bethlehem, others are so zeroed in on his first coming that they forget he has promised to return. Therefore, we ought to be alert, during Advent and after Advent. We ought to "keep awake," remembering that the Father can return home when the Father wants to return home. Keep on the alert!

> To young and old the gospel gladness bear;
> Redeem the time; its hours too swiftly fly.
> The night draws nigh.

> "*Chronos is time measured by humankind.*
> *. . . Kairos is God's time.*"

In the Bible, two words are used to distiguish two different kinds of time. *Chronos* is the time that is running out, the time we often feel that we do not have enough of. It is a measured quantity. *Kairos* is a time of opportunity. It is God's time. *Chronos* is time measured by humankind, a human clock, a human way of bringing order. *Kairos* is God's time, God's way of intervening in our existence and seizing the time, the opportunity. "The hours too swiftly fly" is *chronos* time. On the other hand, our text, "When the right time finally came, God sent his own Son," is *kairos* time. God's intervention is special and can happen at any time. God is hovering over our world, and God picks auspicious times to intervene, which was Arthur Ainger's point when he wrote this poem:

> God is working his purpose out
> as year succeeds to year: . . .
> God is working his purpose out
> and the time is drawing near;
>
> Nearer and nearer draws the time,
> the time that shall surely be,
> when the earth shall be filled
> with the glory of God as the
> waters cover the sea.

There is plenty of time for God's intervention in our world and our lives.

One of President John F. Kennedy's most famous speeches was delivered in West Berlin a few months before his assassination. The climax of that speech came when he said simply and movingly, "I am a Berliner." On the night following his assassination, Germans crowded the streets of West Berlin, and Berliners responded by putting thousands of lights in their windows. Why this dramatic display of affection and grief? Because President Kennedy had identified with them! They had not forgotten that he had claimed to be one of them. He intervened in their difficult history and identified closely with their plight.

Advent begins the season of intervention, of *kairos*, of the time when God changed the direction of humankind for all time by being born into our world. We come humbly and gratefully to his table where he again identified with us in his death. From that cradle and from that cross, Jesus Christ said, "I am one of you."

Keep on the alert, for God can intervene at any time in your life.

> *When the fullness of time had come, God sent his Son. (Gal. 4:4)*

Preparation

*W*e all have stories about how many "close" friends we have. People love to drop in on us and spend a few days once it begins to get cold. It isn't just during the Christmas season that this happens. It happens almost any time during the winter. Isn't it funny that nobody ever drops in to see us during the summer, when you could fry an egg on the sidewalk? Where are all those people then?

We are a nation of transients. People who have not moved within the last eight years have certainly traveled within the last five years. Those who cannot afford vacations for themselves love to see slides of other people's vacations, so they can at least see the world vicariously. Whether we are guests or hosts, being entertained or entertaining, the fact is that most of us enjoy being "on the road again."

Before any trip, large or small, and before the arrival of any visitor, we all must make preparation. I remember one day when my in-laws visited us from Minnesota. We prepared for their arrival by wallpapering the bedroom in which they would be staying. We were going to get around to it some day, but with their approaching arrival, we made that part of our preparation. I had the lawn mowed, we washed the windows, and I cut the hedge.

When they arrived, we were ready for them. My wife had baked for days, so she would not have to do that when they came, and she had the menus pretty well prepared. We had discussed where we might take them. We had prepared well for their arrival.

> ## *"God prepared the world in a unique way for the coming of the Savior."*

Our text from Paul's letter to the church at Galatia reminds us that God was also preparing the world well for the coming of his Son, Jesus: "When the fullness of time had come, God sent his Son" (Gal. 4:4). God didn't just wake up one morning and say, "Well, I think I'll send my Son to the earth today. It's as good a time as any." No, God prepared the world in a unique way for the coming of the Savior.

Scholars have pointed out how the world was prepared by Caesar's great achievement of unification. Then the known world was one empire. There were no known barriers, for the Roman flag flew everywhere on earth.

Because of this there was peace everywhere. If Christ had come a century earlier, the gospel would have been blocked by jealous, national frontiers and with people fighting. If Jesus had come a century later, civilization would have been occupied with the terrible battle against barbarian hordes from the north. But God had prepared the world in such a way that there was for a time world peace, and people would not be distracted by war, but would be able to listen to the gospel.

God also prepared the world by sending Jesus at a time when Rome's great roads were finished. From one end of the empire to the other you could travel on good roads, swiftly and safely. Those who would be spreading the gospel around the world used this means of transportation. Built to carry Caesar's legions, these roads carried God's messengers, and the world was evangelized.

The world was also prepared by the fact that when Jesus was born in Bethlehem there was one common language in the world. Today there are over four thousand languages. When Jesus was born there was one universal language. While each province had its own tongue, everybody everywhere knew Greek, hence the missionaries, as they fanned out along the Roman roads, could evangelize in one language.

Socially, also, the people were ready for a Savior. Two out of every three people in Rome were slaves. One scholar has written that "the disastrous aftermath of war, the wild, colossal extravagance of Herod the Great, the burden of taxation . . . the growing overpopulation which made it impossible for the land to provide food enough for its own inhabitants—these things had precipitated a period of unexampled depression among the great bulk of people" (James S. Stewart, *The Life and Teaching of Jesus Christ* [Nashville: Abingdon Press, 1978], pp. 18-19). People were ready for a change. They longed for someone to save them from the future. They yearned for what the prophets had promised would come out of Bethlehem from the lineage of David. The time had fully come. The way of the Lord had been prepared.

As God prepared the world for the coming of the Christ child, so we now have been given the Advent season, to prepare spiritually for the celebration of God's entering into our world two thousand years ago. Amid all the tinsel, remember that this is what Christmas is. A popular saying conveys a simple message: "Jesus is the reason for the season." Amid all the carols and activity, remember that this is a holy day, not a holiday. This is a time when we should "prepare the way of the Lord." This is a time when we should be growing in our faith and commitment. We should become more loving, more generous to those in and out of our immediate family, more committed to Christ, more eager to help those less fortunate, and bolder in sharing the faith.

As we begin our season of preparation, let us decide now to make it a time of spiritual growth, by planning activities that contribute to our love for one another and our growth in our concern for those less fortunate. One of the best places to begin is at the table of the One who said, "I go to prepare a place for you. And if I go and prepare a place for you, I will come again and will take you to myself, so that where I am, there you may be also" (John 14:2-3).

ADVENT COMMUNION 4

> *All who heard it were amazed at what the shepherds told them. (Luke 2:18)*

Hearers Amazed

Happy New Year! You've heard of the Jewish New Year and the Chinese New Year? Today is the Christian New Year. The Christian faith makes important use of a yearly calendar. At certain times throughout the year we commemorate the great events God has done on our behalf. We have found that celebrating these events on a yearly cycle is spiritually beneficial, for it reminds us of all that God has done and continues to do for us.

Today is the Christian New Year Day because it is the beginning of the Advent season, a four-week period leading up to the celebration of the birth of Jesus Christ. Happy Christian New Year! This is a time for new spiritual beginnings.

One of the most prevalent spiritual difficulties is procrastination. Someday we are going to do what is right. Someday we are going to set the record straight. Someday we are going to give to the church and to the work of Christ as we should. Someday we are going to be loving and kind and considerate and compassionate . . . someday. It is so easy to live in the future and promise to ourselves that someday we will do all the things that we know God wants us to do today. We procrastinate—we put off until tomorrow what we should be doing today.

Advent calls us to a new beginning. The call is to start over again. The call is to prepare our hearts for the new birth of

Christ in the world and a new birth in our own life-style. Thank God we do not have to remain as we always have been. We are called to newness in Christ, and now is the time to respond to that call. "New occasions do teach new duties," as the poet says. "Behold, I have made all things new," says our Lord.

When you think about what could happen to you, you are simply amazed! You could be a different person, a better person. Your friends and your spouse might have a little difficulty dealing with your new self, but they'll adjust. You could settle many of your own problems as you begin this new spiritual year.

It is amazing what could happen to us if we really took seriously this moment and Jesus. Jesus' hearers were continually amazed at what he was doing, and they were always wondering about him. Jesus healed a blind and mute demoniac, and Matthew tells us that "all the crowds were amazed" (12:23). Jesus rebuked an unclean spirit, and he demanded that it come out of a person; it does, and we are told "they were all amazed" (Mark 1:27) Jesus healed a paralyzed man who was lowered through an opening in the roof, and Mark tells us "they were all amazed" (2:12). In another passage we are told, "When the whole crowd saw him, they were immediately overcome with awe." at Jesus' teaching (Mark 9:15). In one verse we even read that the disciples "were perplexed at [his] words" (Mark 10:24).

Again and again Jesus produced wonder and amazement in his hearers, and not just a few, and not just the disciples, but in all his hearers. Pilate "was greatly amazed" at Jesus (Matt. 27:14); "the crowd was amazed" (Matt. 15:31); and again "all spoke well of him and were amazed at the gracious words that came from his mouth" (Luke 4:22). Jesus caused much wonder and considerable head-scratching as he went around preaching the gospel and healing the sick, feeding the hungry, visiting the prisoners, clothing the naked, and giving water to the thirsty. Jesus' new way of life had all the people wondering: Who is this man called Jesus? Where did he come from? What in the world is he up to? Is he for real? What if I really committed myself to following him? What would happen to me and mine?

We shouldn't be too surprised at these reactions, for these were the reactions he got from the time of his birth. This attitude of amazement was an early response to him, as our text from Luke indicates. When the shepherds went to Bethlehem and told everybody what had happened to them out in the field, "All who heard it were amazed at what the shepherds told them." From the very beginning, even as an infant, Jesus set people to wondering about him.

Nowhere does the Bible promise that all people will follow Jesus. Nowhere does the Bible promise that all people will love Jesus. Nowhere does the Bible promise that Jesus will have an easy time living in our world. But isn't it suggestive to hear that the Bible does indicate that Jesus will set all people to wondering about him? He will challenge the thinking of all of us. He will attack our indifference. He will call for our commitment of resources. He will ask for our loyalty. He will demand our love. Not all people will respond favorably, but all people will wonder . . . "Should I . . . ? Dare I? If I do, what then?"

Some of you are still wondering about Jesus. Many of you will just keep on wondering, but some will move beyond wondering and will commit (or recommit) yourselves. You will stop procrastinating.

> *Jesus produces wonder and amazement during Advent.*

I like George Beverly Shea. I guess I grew up listening to that big voice of his, and as a teenager, with my own changing voice, I always hoped that my voice would someday settle near his range. (It never did.) But when he sings, even to this day, I listen. Here is one of my favorites that he sings:

> There's the wonder of sunset at evening,
> The wonder as sunrise I see;
> But the wonder of wonders that thrills my soul
> Is the wonder that God loves me.
>
> There's the wonder of spring time and harvest,
> The sky, the stars, the sun;
> But the wonder of wonders that thrills my soul
> Is the wonder that's only begun.
>
> O, the wonder of it all! The wonder of it all!
> Just to think that God loves me.
> O, the wonder of it all! The wonder of it all!
> Just to think that God loves me.
>
> ("The Wonder of It All")*

The first Sunday in the Advent season, the Sacrament of Holy Communion, is a new beginning, a time for a new you. Let us leave behind the crowd that is committed to wondering about Jesus, for we are called to be among the few who move from wondering to commitment to Jesus. The wonder of it all is that God loves us! Happy New Year! Happy new you!

---

*"The Wonder of It All" by George Beverly Shea. Copyright © 1957 by Chancel Music, Inc. Assigned to The Rodeheaver Company. © Renewed 1985 by The Rodeheaver Co. (a division of Word, Inc.). All rights reserved. International copyright secured. Used by permission.

> *For a thousand years in your sight*
> *are like yesterday when it is past,*
> *or like a watch in the night. (Psalm 90:4)*

How Time Flies

P salm 90 is one of the most beloved psalms and the only one attributed to Moses. Scholars have called it a "precious gem," while many people have requested it at their funeral, on their tombstone, or have written it into the literature of their day.

"We ponder God's eternity."

Isaac Watts, the famous hymn writer, is no exception. Inspired by its eloquence and, at the same time, its spiritual depth, he wrote on the eternity of God and the mortality of humankind. Listen for this theme:

> O God, our help in ages past,
> our hope for years to come,
> our shelter from the stormy blast,
> and our eternal home!
>
> Before the hills in order stood,
> or earth received her frame,
> from everlasting, thou art God,
> to endless years the same.

A thousand ages, in thy sight,
are like an evening gone;
short as the watch that ends the night,
before the rising sun.

Time, like an ever rolling stream,
bears all who breathe away;
they fly forgotten, as a dream
dies at the opening day.

O God, our help in ages past,
our hope for years to come;
be thou our guide while life shall last,
and our eternal home.

We ponder God's eternity as we hover on the edge of a new year. On New Year's Eve, on our birthday, and maybe when we are ill and have to take care of our bodies, we especially are conscious of time passing. The newspapers and the magazines have all been carrying articles about the important events of the past year. We are but a few hours from a new year, and soon the year 2000 will be here. My high school history teacher impressed on us students that one day everyone in the class would be alive to usher in the year 2000. Most of us laughed because it sounded so funny. But it will soon come to pass.

Amid all the changes and the passing of time, we have God's eternity. Said the psalmist:

> Lord, you have been our dwelling place
> in all generations.
> Before the mountains were brought forth
> or even you had formed the
> earth and the world,
> from everlasting to everlasting
> you are God. (Ps. 90:1-2)

The second letter of Peter says, "But do not ignore this one fact, beloved, that with the Lord one day is like a thousand years, and a thousand years are like one day" (II Pet. 3:8). God's eternity is sometimes hard for us to grasp.

33

> ## "Contrast God's eternity to our mortality."

There is a legend that high up in the north in the land of Suitjod there stands a rock that is one hundred miles high and one hundred miles wide. Once every thousand years a little bird comes to this rock to sharpen its beak. When the rock has thus been worn away, then a single day of eternity will have gone by, says the legend. Can you feel how long eternity is? God operates with that kind of perspective.

> For a thousand years in your sight
> are like yesterday when it is past,
> or like a watch in the night. (Ps. 90:4)

God is the alpha and the omega, the beginning and the end.

Now contrast God's eternity to our mortality, God's infiniteness and our finiteness, God's unlimitedness and our limitedness.

> You sweep them away; they are like a dream,
> like grass that is renewed in the morning;
> in the morning it flourishes and is renewed;
> in the evening it fades and withers. (Ps. 90:5-6)

The Bible is expressing what we all should know. We aren't going to be on this earth forever, and so, we had better get our lives, our morals, our values, our goals, and our destination in focus. Certainly New Year's Eve reminds us of this. The psalmist says, "Teach us to count our days that we may gain a wise heart" (90:12).

New Year's Eve is a good time to take inventory. While many will be trying their best to hide their mortality this evening in parties and alcoholic binges, we have chosen to contemplate our mortality and God's eternity. What does it mean to be on this earth for a limited number of days? How many days are really left? What about our loved ones? Can we really turn our lives around tonight? Can we really resolve to be more Christlike in our lives and make it stick?

Eric Severeid, during a question-and-answer period following a rather depressing lecture, was asked, "What, then, gives you hope?" He responded, "We are all trapped somewhere between earth and a glimpse of heaven, and I try not to lose that glimpse." Tonight, we get a glimpse of heaven in this sacrament. Do you see it?

> *There will be more joy in heaven over one sinner who repents than over ninety-nine righteous persons who need no repentance. (Luke 15:7)*

Party of One

Many experiences in life are by definition isolated ones that we will all experience. They are lonely experiences. Illness is an experience that we cannot share with anyone else. Our own sickness and mortality isolate us from others, even our loved ones. We have to face death as individuals. Alone! No one can join us in our death. Others can be with us to the end, but we must "cross the bar" alone. Birthdays can also be lonely experiences, especially as we mature, for birthdays remind us that time is passing and that we have a few more "silver threads among the gold."

Even New Year's Eve is a rather isolating experience. Some of you came here tonight with family and friends. Even if you came alone, you are now among church family and friends, so in one sense you are not entering the new year alone. But in a more profound sense, you are, because just as you entered life alone, as you grow older on your birthday alone, as you experience illness alone, so also must you enter the new year alone.

> *"Many people are having their annual end-of-the-year crisis."*

I think some of the revelry tonight, some of the drunkenness, some of the horseplay that goes on is evidence that many people are having their annual end-of-the-year crisis. "Another year has passed and I am one year closer to. . . . What? I don't want to think about it. I had better party and drink and not think. Turn up the music."

One of the most popular activities on New Year's Eve is eating out. Have you ever gone out by yourself and arrived at the door of the restaurant, to be greeted by someone who asks how many are in your party? You respond, almost with embarrassment, "Only one." "A party of one," she will say. "Please follow me." When this happens to me, I always feel a little funny. Here I am all alone. Don't I have any friends? Why do I have to eat alone? Look at all the people eating with other people, and I'm not. Sometimes just eating alone can be an isolating experience.

I like that phrase "a party of one," and I would recommend the concept to you for next year. What I like is the idea that one person is enough to have a party. A party's success is not determined by how many attend or by who attends. You are a party of one in the eyes of God. You don't have to be with anyone else or be anywhere else or do anything else other than be yourself. You are a whole party all wrapped up in yourself. God will not love you any more when you do more, eat more, go out more, drink more, give more, worship more, than God loves you right now. All by yourself you are a party of one. You are a celebration!

Luke 15 reminds us of this fact: "Which one of you, having a hundred sheep and losing one of them, does not leave the ninety-nine in the wilderness and go after the one that is lost until he finds it?" (Luke 15:4). While many people are interested in numbers and dollars and size, God is interested in individuals. Then Jesus adds a theological interpretation, just in case his listener, or in this case we, miss the point. "Just so, I tell you, there will be more joy in heaven over one sinner who repents than over ninety-nine righteous persons who need no repentance" (Luke 15:7).

Notice two points from this passage of Scripture. First, it should be obvious that "only one" is enough. We do not need to make any kind of excuse when we are alone. "Who's there?" "Just me!" "That's enough!" We can lift our heads high and walk erect and not be ashamed when we travel life alone. There is nothing wrong with a person who is alone or who is seeking solitude. God loves the one as much as the ninety-nine. God listens for the one as much as he listens for the ninety-nine. Your one voice, your one concern, your one prayer, your one hurt, your one sorrow are enough to turn God's head from the masses and say, "I hear you, loved one, I hear you." Never apologize for being only one. One is enough.

Second, not only is one enough, but also one is a party. It is a celebration. It is a New Year's celebration. Tonight we have come to celebrate. This is the celebration of the sacrament of Holy Communion. This is a reverent party given by Jesus Christ for our benefit on New Year's Eve. The beauty of our party is that there will be no hangover on the day after. Rather than remorse and guilt on the day after, we will feel confidence and spiritual vigor. We will have release from the burden of our sins. We will know the forgiveness that only God can provide.

Tomorrow we will look back on this New Year's Eve celebration with joy and pride, knowing that we ended the old year in worship and began the New Year in praise. Let us then prepare to participate in this party of one, the celebration of the sacrament of Holy Communion.

> *Since, therefore, the children share flesh and blood, he himself likewise shared the same things, so that through death he might destroy the one who has the power of death, that is, the devil. (Heb. 2:14)*

An Inquiline God

I always knew there was a pope in Rome, but now I know it for a fact, because he has visited the United States, and I saw him on television as he visited Boston, New York, Miami, and other places. It was so refreshing to see pictures of him embracing people and being quoted on the front pages, talking about our need to love one another and that we should oppose war and that we must strive to save life in this world. For many of us, the pope came alive as we saw him daily in living color on our televisions.

Yet, he was always alive, always active, always embracing people, always talking about love and condemning hate. The difference is that he was now in our country, walking on our soil, talking in our language, sharing with thousands as they stood in the rain together celebrating what we call the sacrament of Holy Communion. He had become one of us, visiting small rural churches and large million-dollar cathedrals. He was now more human. He knew our way of life and some of the peculiar temptations that Americans live with daily.

When Albert Einstein came to Princeton, New Jersey, in 1934, everyone who got to know him was enchanted at what a man of simplicity and almost saintliness he was. He lived in an unpretentious house on a side street near the seminary. It is said that he could often be seen sitting reading on his front porch on a warm afternoon. One day a neighboring woman was horrified to discover that Einstein had been helping her ten-year-old daughter with arithmetic homework every afternoon as she would stop by his house on her way home from school. The mother scolded her child for bothering the great man. The girl replied, "He likes me, and when he explains about numbers I can understand." The man who had conceived the theory of relativity came across to a ten-year-old as a loving man who made sense out of the confusions of elementary mathematics. He spoke her language.

This, too, was the genius of God in Jesus Christ—he who shared in the infinities of eternity, where creation was conceived, came across to ordinary people as a loving person who made sense out of the confusions of life. Jesus became like us and shared our human nature. "He had to become like his brothers and sisters in every respect, so that he might be a merciful and faithful high priest in the service of God, to make a sacrifice of atonement for the sins of the people. Because he himself was tested by what he suffered, he is able to help those who are being tested" (Hebrews 2:17-18).

Inquiline is the word. It literally means an animal that lives in the nest of another. I must admit that I had never heard of the word until I read in *The Clergy Journal* about an organization called Inquiline. It is a house-swapping service, which will list your house in its digest for fifteen dollars. A digest entry describes the owner's house, sometimes including all the furniture, and gives a preferred swap location. Usually Californians want to swap with East Coasters or Europeans. For nervous swappers, and for an extra fee, Inquiline can arrange to give the swappers a report on the family who will be living in their house.

We have an inquiline God. God has chosen to become identified with our world and "live in our nest," and in Jesus

Christ came to live with us. This idea was in stark contrast to the Greek idea of God, which was that the gods were detached and unmoved by the events that transpired on the earth. The Greeks' conception of their gods was similar to the way Tennyson pictures them in "The Song of the Lotus Eaters":

> For they lie beside their nectar, and the bolts are hurl'd
> Far below them in the valleys, and the clouds are lightly
>   curl'd
> Round their golden houses, girdled with the gleaming
>   world:
> Where they smile in secret, looking over wasted lands,
> Blight and famine, plague and earthquake, roaring deeps
>   and fiery sands,
> Clanging fights, and flaming towns, and sinking ships, and
>   praying hands.

Detached and far removed are the Greek gods. Not so the Christlike God whose very essence was the identification of God with humankind. God came to live in our "nest." God chose to identify with us in Jesus Christ. God cared enough to send his very best, to live in our nest, to be inquiline.

During World War II, when the Nazi armies were in almost every country of Europe, King Christian of Denmark stubbornly resisted the Nazis. His country was quite small compared to powerful Germany, and the king knew he could not win on the battlefield, but he put up a valiant moral struggle. One day he observed a Nazi flag flying above one of his public buildings. He reminded the German commander that this was contrary to the treaty between the two nations, and he said, "The flag must be removed before 12 o'clock; otherwise I will send a soldier to remove it." At five minutes before 12:00, the flag was still flying, and the king announced that he was sending a soldier to take it down. "The soldier will be shot," the Nazi officer replied. Then King Christian calmly said, "I think I should tell you that I will be that soldier."

God so loved the whole world that when he saw the flag of disobedience and hatred, jealousy and strife, selfishness and greed flying over our public and private lives, he called for its removal. When we responded by saying, "We shall kill whomever you send to remove this flag," God said, "I think I should tell you that I will come myself in Jesus Christ."

And so, on this New Year's Eve Communion we gather to celebrate a God who identified so closely with the whole world that he became one of us even unto death so that we might begin anew.

NEW YEAR COMMUNION 4

> *So if anyone is in Christ, there is a new creation: everything old has passed away; see, everything has become new! (II Cor. 5:17)*

How to Get There

During the Korean War a captain had his headquarters behind the front lines. One day, as the captain was working in his tent, a corporal came rushing in. He looked dirty and battle weary as he breathlessly reported, "Sir, I need your help. I have a problem." The captain responded, "What is your problem?" The soldier replied, "Sir, my men are pinned down with sniper fire; they've been abandoned. They have had no food for three days, and we need to send a rescue party. If not, we'll lose the territory and the men." The captain said, "I hear you."

At the same moment, another corporal rushed into the tent and said, "Sir, I have a problem." And the captain asked, "What is your problem?" The corporal said, "Sir, my tent leaks."

As we hover on the brink of a new year, I would like to offer the suggestion that we can tell much about ourselves by the kind of life we lived in the previous year. Certainly we can look back and see a track record that adds up to a certain value system. Was it a year to be proud of? Was it a year to be ashamed of? Was it a year in which nothing much happened in your life? Was it a year that, if you had a chance, you would live all over again? Someone once said that we can tell a lot about ourselves by looking at our old check stubs. Look not only at your check stubs for last year, but also look at how you invested your time and energy. Does it express the kind of person you want to be when you are your best self?

"My tent leaks."

What kind of problems have you been concerned with in the year that just ended? Have they been tent-leaking problems, or life-and-death issues? Tell me what some of your problems were, and I will tell you about yourself. Some of us have been worried over the number of people who have suffered in the last twelve months. We are concerned that others might develop a "compassion fatigue" and turn a cold shoulder to those in need. We have worried about war and energy supplies. We have worried about hundreds of thousands of earthquake victims. We have worried about victims of hurricanes and tornadoes. We have worried about hungry people and the fact that ten thousand died of starvation every day last year. We worry that four thousand abortions were performed every day. We worry about the fact that millions of people do not have a decent shelter or education for their children. We worry about those who have more than enough to live on and will not share.

These were the problems, the worries of some, while others worried about the condition of their second and third homes or the deteriorating condition of their boats. Some worried about their grass, and some worried about how they might go on another cruise. Others have worried about their stocks. Tell me what you have been worrying about, tell me what your problems have been, and I will know a great deal about you.

As we prepare to enter a new year by taking the sacrament of Holy Communion, our text reminds us that newness begins inside us. Newness begins with a renewing of our spirits by the Holy Spirit. "If anyone is in Christ, there is a new creation. . . . " This is where it all begins. It doesn't begin with a shower and a shave. It doesn't begin with a new hairdo. We don't need a whitewash on the outside. We need a cleansing on the inside.

On December 13, 1988, the Fort Lauderdale *Sun-Sentinel* carried the obituaries of two men who on the outside looked about the same, but what a difference there was on the inside! Anthony Provenzano was a Hallandale, Florida, resident who died while serving twenty years for a 1979 racketeering conviction. "Tony Pro," as he was known in the Mafia, was reputed to be the one who had Jimmy Hoffa killed and was allegedly a soldier in the Genovese organized crime family.

On the same page, right next to his obituary, was that of Lawrence A. Wien, from Palm Beach and New York, who in 1982 said he had already provided a reasonable degree of security for his family, and so, he "decided to have the fun of giving my money away." And that's just what he did—to the arts, and to civic, educational, and welfare organizations. He called his philosophy of giving "intelligent selfishness," stating that he wanted to see the results of his giving while he was alive.

Some of his biggest gifts included $8.5 million to Brandeis University and $20 million to his alma mater, Columbia University. Before he died he had a profound influence on many educational institutions and many fine arts programs, and hence, on thousands of people. What had Tony Pro done? You tell me! Two men whose obituaries appeared on the same day, in the same paper, on the same page, side by side, but oh, what a difference in their lives, because their inner lives were different.

If anyone is in Christ, there is a new creation: everything old has passed away; see, everything has become new!

Where do you want to go in the new year? How will you get there? If you want to grow spiritually, you have come to the right place. This is the place that God has established for those who want to be better Christians. If that's where you'd like to be a year from now, you have come to the right location. This is God's "growing place."

In T. S. Eliot's "Choruses from 'The Rock,' " he asked some good questions to ponder on New Year's Eve.

> Where is the Life we have lost in living?
> Where is the wisdom we have lost in knowledge?
> Where is the knowledge we have lost in information? . . .

Eliot's solution? "The Church must be forever building, for it is forever decaying within and attacked from without."

As you partake of Christ's body and blood, know that it can build you into a brand-new person on the inside.

> *So we do not lose heart. Even though our outer nature is wasting away, our inner nature is being renewed day by day. (II Cor. 4:16)*

Where Is My Life Going?

C an you believe it? Another whole year has just zoomed past us. Three hundred and sixty-five days. Fifty-two weeks. Time really does fly! It is New Year's Eve again. It seems as if we just had a New Year's Eve Communion service. Some of you were here last year. Doesn't it seem as if we just had this service?

> Forenoon and afternoon and night,—
> Forenoon,
> And afternoon, and night. . . .
> Yea, that is Life.
> (Edward Rowland Sill, "Life")

In the twinkling of an eye I will be standing here on the brink of another year. Where is my life going?

The swift passing of time is not an experience unique to the 1990s. The psalmist made reference to it: "For a thousand years in your sight are like yesterday when it is past, or like a watch in the night" (Ps. 90:4). Poet Richard Burton wrote:

> If I had the time to find a place
> And sit me down full face to face
> With my better self, that cannot show
> In my daily life that rushes so:

It might be then I would see my soul
Was stumbling still toward the shining goal,
I might be nerved by the thought sublime,—
If I had the time!

("If We Had the Time")

Where is my life going? The Apostle Paul in our Scripture lesson helps to put the whole thing in perspective. He reminds us that our bodies are only earthen vessels. He reminds us that in this life we can count on affliction, confusion, persecution, and even being struck down. But he also reminds us that the purpose of life and all of this difficulty is "so that the life of Jesus may be made visible in our mortal flesh" (II Cor. 4:11). Paul, the man with the thorn in the flesh, who prayed that it might be removed and found out that it was never going to be, had to come to grips with passing time and an aging body. There must have been times when he raised the same question, "Where is my life going? It is all going by so fast, and there is so much to do for Christ. So many people with whom to share the good news."

But then, having thought about it, he came to the conclusion that is found in our text: "So we do not lose heart. Even though our outer nature is wasting away, our inner nature is being renewed day by day." Paul felt time passing. He felt the frustration of not having enough time to get everything done. He saw his life slipping through his fingers, but he did not lose heart. Other translators say that Paul never gave up, and he never became discouraged.

In other words, he admitted that from a human point of view life could be rather discouraging. But he hastened to add that we have more than human ingenuity and strength going for us. We have the transcending power that belongs to God and not to us.

> "Concentrate on the growth of the inner nature."

The key to successful Christian living now and in the year ahead is to concentrate on the growth of the inner nature and not the outer nature. The deterioration of the outer nature is something about which we can do nothing. The growth of the inner nature is something about which we can do everything.

Where is my life going physically? To the grave! That's the fact. I came fully to grips with this fact one summer and bought a plot of earth in which to deposit my body when I am finished with it. I want to give it a decent burial, for it is serving me well. Some want to be cremated, and that's fine also. This outer nature is going to disappear, but my inner nature is a different matter. The Quaker adage says it well: "By God's grace I'm going to really live until I die; and then, I'm going to live forever." At death we who are in communion with God through Jesus Christ are going to shed our bodies, which by then will have become somewhat of a burden anyway.

God loves us for a purpose— "so that everyone who believes in [Jesus Christ] may not perish but may have eternal life" (John 3:16). The body will be gone. But the soul will have eternal life, if our inner nature has been renewed through contact with the Holy Spirit.

Tonight we gather here, not to eat; there is hardly enough food on the table to satisfy one of us. We are here to satisfy our souls. We are here to renew our inner natures. We are here to keep the real person alive. We are here to nourish the real us, as we enter a new year together. Through this sacrament, God has promised to renew our inner spirit.

My, my, my. Where is my life going? The real me is going directly to God!

LENTEN COMMUNION 1

> *Examine yourselves, and only then eat of the bread and drink of the cup. (I Cor. 11:28)*

Nearer, My God, to Thee

During the Lenten season—the forty days plus the Sundays before Easter, when we are most eager to advance our spiritual growth—we look again at what we believe and what the consequences of those beliefs might be. As we think about the sacrament of Holy Communion, consider the words of Sarah F. Adams:

> Nearer, my God, to thee, nearer to thee!
> E'en though it be a cross that raiseth me;
> Still all my song shall be, nearer, my God, to thee
> Nearer, my God, to thee, nearer to thee!

The first purpose of the sacrament of Holy Communion is to bring God closer to us and to bring us closer to God. Jesus Christ is the Word made flesh. He is the incarnation of the living God. We are reenacting his death on the cross every time we break this bread and pour this cup, for it was on that cross that his body was broken and his blood poured.

The words of Scripture from I Corinthians are actually the first recorded words that we possess of Jesus Christ on any sub-

ject, for this letter to the church in Corinth is older than the
Gospels of Matthew, Mark, Luke, and John. Jesus said, "This is
my body that is for you. Do this in remembrance of me. . . .
This cup is the new covenant in my blood. Do this, as often as
you drink it, in remembrance of me" (I Cor. 11:24-25).

> Be known to us in breaking bread,
> But do not then depart;
> Saviour, abide with us, and spread
> Thy table in our heart.
> (James Montgomery)

Your prayer, as you eagerly anticipate the distribution of
the bread and wine should be, "Kum ba yah, my Lord, kum
ba yah" ("Come by here, my Lord, come by here"). But we
might ask, what is it that we believe is going to "kum ba yah"?
There are many different beliefs surrounding the sacrament
of Holy Communion.

We know, for example, that Roman Catholics believe that
Jesus Christ is physically present in the bread and wine. That is
why, when they enter the sanctuary of a Roman Catholic
church, the faithful walk down the aisle and then cross themselves and kneel before they enter a pew. This is a proper
acknowledgment that Jesus Christ is as physically present with
them that day as their priest is physically present. It is only
right and proper, if that were our belief, that we should in
some way acknowledge Jesus' presence with us. To the Roman
Catholics, Jesus is really physically present in the bread and
wine. Oh, it might look like bread and wine, and it might taste
like bread and wine, but underneath the "breadness" and the
"wineness" is the real physical presence of Jesus Christ.

Protestants have wrestled with the meaning of the Lord's
Supper. With various nuances, we Protestants have affirmed
that this meal has a symbolic and memorial purpose. Some of
us find Christ more present in our hearts and minds as we
partake of the fruit of the vine and the bread. Some of us prefer
to think of the service as a remembrance, as a simple memo-

rial. It is like remembering Martin Luther King, Jr., on his national holiday, the third Monday of January. We do not claim he is physically with us, but we do remember what he stood for.

Now, in between these two theological wings of Christendom is another large segment of Protestantism. They believe that Jesus Christ is present, but spiritually present, not limited to being in the bread and wine, but through the bread and wine he is present only to those who have faith.

Now all of those concepts are important. Jesus Christ is really with us. He is really present, but not physically present in the bread and wine. If we spill the wine, we have not spilled the blood of Jesus Christ. Jesus is spiritually present in the bread and wine. The nearness of God, which we pray for and can expect, is the real spiritual presence of Jesus Christ through the bread and wine to everyone who has faith in the saving power of Christ.

> *"This sacrament is reserved for only one kind of people: sinners."*

Let's look at our text again, for it demands that we examine ourselves, and only then should we eat this bread and drink from this cup. Have you done that yet? A Scottish minister saw one Sunday morning an elderly woman who hesitated and actually refused to receive the cup. He took her hand and said to her, "Take it, woman; it's for sinners; it's for you." This sacrament is reserved for only one kind of people: sinners. Our text, demanding of us a thorough spiritual examination, does not mean that we should not receive it if we are sinners. If it did, no one would be allowed to partake.

Our text reminds us that we need to come with the attitude of a repentant sinner, of a person who has fallen short of the glory of God and who will from now on seek to be a better person. We need the attitude of one who wants to be better after we have communed. We need the attitude of one who admits he or she has not been loving enough or forgiving enough or compassionate enough or has not sought justice enough. We are sorry for that, and now we would seek to do better.

The old gospel tune puts it a little bluntly, but accurately, when it says:

> Would you be free from your burden of sin? . . .
> Would you be free from your passion and pride? . . .
> There's wonderful pow'r in the Blood.

That power resides in the blood and body of Jesus, through the bread and wine of Holy Communion. Let us now draw nearer to God and receive his wonderful power.

> *Examine yourselves, and only then eat of the bread and drink of the cup. (I Cor. 11:28)*

Take a Look

A man died. He was known for his wild living. When his will was read, it was discovered that he had willed his farm to the devil. The courts, deliberating on such a ridiculous set of circumstances, decided that the best way to carry out his wishes was to let the farm grow up in weeds and briars, to allow the houses and barns to remain unpainted and to rot, and to permit the soil to erode and wash away. The court said, "The best way to let Satan have it is to do nothing with it."

Isn't that the truth with an individual life? Isn't it true of your life? All that is needed for a life to go downhill spiritually is for a person to neglect his or her spiritual side, the most important side. You don't even have to make a great ringing declaration about your future intentions. All you have to do is stop taking care of your spiritual life to see how quickly your spiritual home collapses, your spiritual roots decay, and the weeds of sin prosper.

> *"We give our spiritual life benign neglect."*

I'm convinced that nobody ever really declares that he or she is going to live the life of an atheist. Few, if any, of us really come to a conscious decision to turn our backs on Christ and God's church. I don't think we really look at the Bible and say that it is of no help to us, that prayer is a waste of time, and that worship is unnecessary. We just neglect them and let the devil take over our lives by default. We give our spiritual life benign neglect.

God knows this. God has been around long enough so that we can pull very few surprises. That is why God keeps giving us opportunities to reexamine our direction in life. Life is full of these kinds of opportunities that in the normal course of events introduce a sober thought to our minds, no matter how shallow we may be living.

One of these times is when we are ill. We wonder about pain and why we were born and what death is like. When we leave home, we discover another time for self-examination: Who am I without my family? Does God live everywhere? When we get married and become parents, we seem to have more inner questions: What kind of husband or wife am I going to be? What kind of mother or father will I be? Am I being all that I want to be? Should I change what I have been? If so, how? The whole maturing process is geared toward self-examination from childhood, through adolescence, young adulthood, middle age, and old age. Today, I'm personally discovering that middle age has its own times of self-examination and reflection.

When my father had a series of strokes, I had many spiritual questions. This is one of those "normal" experiences in life that call for self-examination. These are God-given opportunities, not to be feared or ignored, but to be grasped and used for our own growth. Someone has rightly said that an unexamined life is no life at all.

Our text tells us to "examine ourselves" before we "eat of the bread and drink of the cup," lest we bring judgment upon ourselves. How's your examination coming? What kind of tests are you administering? What kind of goals are you establishing? How are you measuring your progress? What kind of life will you lead after your self-examination?

55

> *"A love feast . . . was being used as a divisive tool."*

The poor Corinthian church was greatly in need of this call for self-examination by Paul, for they were in the midst of a feud. For a number of generations after Christ, the Lord's Supper was observed not as part of a formal religious service at Sunday worship, but as the climax of a common meal together, a meal much like the covered-dish supper today. Each family brought food to be shared. Some were poor, and some were rich, but all shared equally, except in Corinth. The rich, who could arrive early, since they were their own bosses, were gathering early in cliques and eating alone and sharing their fancy contributions of food only with one another. The poor, mainly slaves, arrived with their humble contributions after they had done their day's work, and so were forced to eat only their own food. In other words, a love feast that was meant to be shared with the whole Christian community, so that rich and poor, master and slave, would be together, was being used as a divisive tool. Christian fellowship was not being served by the meal; it was being severed. In addition, many were finishing the meal in a state of alcoholic stupor, so that they were drunk when it came time for the Lord's Supper to be celebrated. The Corinthian church was being selfish, gluttonous, and was eating the Lord's Supper in an irreverent manner, as if it was meant only to be another meal. Examine yourselves, they were told, in the light of what you are doing.

At the conclusion of some celebrations of the Lord's Supper, the minister turns to the people and proclaims, "Now you are the body of Christ." That is a good thought, for when we eat this bread and drink from this cup, these elements enter our bodies and literally become a part of us. They go into our blood stream and travel to our brains, our hearts, our sinews, and our muscles. The body and blood of Christ become incorporated into our own body and blood. Thus we become in the process a part of him. We take him, his life, his death, his resurrection into our very selves, into our own lives and deaths and even rising. Now we are the body of Christ, and now we are meant to be a Christ to our neighbors.

Someone has suggested that every college graduate should be examined every five years to see whether she or he still deserves the degree. We Christians should be examining ourselves regularly to see whether we still deserve the degree of "Christian." Are we moving in the right direction? Are we striving to be better people? Are we taking advantage of opportunities for growth?

Let's take a look! This is one of those God-given opportunities for spiritual self-examination. Let's examine ourselves. We don't have to be perfect, but we should be trying, striving, moving in the direction of Christ. For now we are the body of Christ on this earth. Jesus said, "This is my body, broken for you. This is my blood, shed for you, and when you eat this, I become part of you and you become part of me."

> *If I ascend to heaven, you are there; if I make my bed in Sheol, you are there. (Ps. 139:8)*

No Escape from Life

It may seem strange that during Lent, when we think about New Testament events, such as the life, death, and resurrection of Jesus Christ, I have chosen to preach a sermon on one of the most popular books of the Old Testament. But there is a definite relationship between the two.

Dr. Patrick Miller, in his book *Interpreting the Psalms*, wrote:

> The Psalms draw us to Jesus, make us think of Him; they gain their specificity, their reality for us, their concreteness, in the revelation of Jesus . . . the Psalms provide some of the fundamental content for what the reality of Jesus is as salvation, light, hope, deliverance, Shepherd . . . it is surely the case that to the extent that Jesus is the answer, one must have heard what the questions are [in the Psalms].

This is why I think a sermon on the psalms during the Lenten season is appropriate, for the human cries and questions raised by the psalmist are answered by God in the life of Christ, and especially by Christ's death and resurrection.

> *"Now we are going to take a little vacation from the divine."*

The psalmist, in our text, raises the practical question, "Can I ever escape from God?" For many, it is comforting to know that no matter how bad things get, God is there. No matter where you find yourself, no matter how far down you have sunk, no matter where you end up, God is there with you. It is a reassuring theme.

But others look at this text from a different slant. We want to get away from God. We've had it with God. We are not happy with the way things in life are going, and now we are going to take a little vacation from the divine to see how things work out. In reality, we would be glad to escape from God, and maybe even from the responsibilities in life that God has given us. If you find yourself thinking such thoughts, then you are having a common human experience. Many of us are eager to retreat from life and escape from our present surroundings.

One scholar wrote that many of us long for a way of escape from the adult responsibilities of life by escaping back into our childhood. Actually this is the essence of schizophrenia, a regression to childhood. For all of us, childhood is a symbol of the comfort and protection of our parents, and all the carefree hours seem, in our memory, to have been filled with innocent joys.

> Backward, flow backward, O tide of the years!
> I am so weary of toil and of tears,—
> Toil without recompense, tears all in vain,—
> Take them, and give me my childhood again!
> (Elizabeth Akers, "Rock Me to Sleep")

Some of the best-known people in the Bible were almost overwhelmed by their predicaments and were certainly ready to quit. King David cried out, "O that I had wings like a dove! I would fly away, and be at rest" (Ps. 55:6). He had good reason for wanting to flee from Jerusalem, because there was serious trouble in his kingdom. His own son was leading a rebellion against him. Instead of loyalty and love, he was greeted with hatred. Lawlessness and violence were running rampant in the streets of his own capital city. As he brooded on his troubles, he became panicstricken. His heart was rent with anguish, and fear and trembling overwhelmed him. He wanted out. He searched for a way of escape. "O that I had wings like a dove! Let me out of here!"

Elijah, stronghearted though he was, panicked in the face of the enemy and fled into the wilderness. Cowering under a broom tree, he prayed: "It is enough; now, O LORD, take away my life, for I am no better than my ancestors" (I Kings 19:4).

Jeremiah, made sick at heart by the sins of his people and oppressed by life's burdens, cried:

> O that I had in the desert
> a traveler's lodging place,
> that I might leave my people
> and go away from them! (Jer. 9:2)

And the Apostle Paul, in a moment of discouragement, declared: "I am hard pressed between the two: my desire is to depart and be with Christ, for that is far better" (Phil. 1:23).

Who of us, on occasion, has not wished for David's "wings like a dove" in order to escape, or Elijah's "broom tree" in order to hide, or Jeremiah's "traveler's lodging place" in order to relax? The psalmist, in our text, was experiencing such a time also, but he discovered that no matter where he went, God was there, ahead of him, with him, and after him. No matter where we flee God has been there, God is there, and God will be there again.

The clear message of the incarnation, of God's visiting us in the flesh, is that we cannot escape God. God pursues us.

God dwells with us. God is with us, like a mother hen looking after her chicks, says the Bible.

> ## "What happens when I fall short of God's expectation of me?"

And what about our final experience, death? What happens when I have not lived up to my potential? What happens if I have spent for my own benefit most of what God has given me? What if I have lacked Christian love for people different from me? What happens when I fall short of God's expectation of me? The psalmist assures us that God will not leave us. Jesus' sacrifice on the cross, symbolized in this Communion, tells us that he is with us even in death, for he has gone through a physical death ahead of us. Jesus knows exactly what we will go through, and he will be with you.

The Soviet Union has had a sordid history of imprisoning its own people for doing things that we in the United States take for granted. The biggest crime most of them committed was to have disagreed with their government. One man spent nine long years in prison, but he had one steady companion all that time: his psalm book! Most of his other possessions were taken away from him, but he clung to his miniature copy of the psalms, which his wife had sent him.

In fact, this man once spent 130 days (over four months) in solitary confinement because he refused to allow the authorities to confiscate his psalm book. Why? Because reading the familiar old songs of agony and faith, doubt and courage, gave him the strength to go on during his long ordeal. He knew in his darkest moments that God was with him. God does not want us to escape from life; God wants us to face it, and when we do, God promises to be right there alongside us. There is no escape from life or from God. Thank God!

God, in Christ, committed himself to life and death for us. Going to the cross, he discovered that there is no escape from life. Now, offering to us this sacrament of Holy Communion, he calls us to live life to the fullest. Try not to escape.

LENTEN COMMUNION 4

> *We find nothing wrong with this man. (Acts 23:9)*

What's Wrong with You?

I t's the basic question of life: What's wrong with you? Sometimes the question is asked in this way, "What's wrong with *you?*" Here it is made to sound as if there was something uniquely ajar in you that is not so in me. This question can be asked in such a way to suggest that "I'm okay; you're not okay." "What's wrong with *you?* You've got problems, fellow, that I don't have. Poor, miserable you. Lucky, fortunate me."

When the question is asked that way, excessive arrogance is associated with it. I feel superior to another person and imply that if the other person would only be like me, then every thing would be normal. In this moment, I become the standard for normalcy. Those persons who measure up to me have nothing wrong with them. What about those persons who don't measure up? They need help.

As we continue our spiritual pilgrimage of forty days until Easter, I would like us to put the emphasis elsewhere in the question: "What's *wrong* with you?" By this I mean that you are not spiritually unique in this matter at all. You and I have the same "wrongness" in us, and we have the same degree of difficulty in handling it. "What's *wrong* with you?" means that all of us have something ajar, something out of line, something off track in our lives. We all have this "wrongness" in common.

> ## *"We all have this 'wrongness' in common."*

Several years ago *Time* magazine had a cover story on the actor Peter Sellers. When he appeared on "The Muppet Show," he was told by Kermit the Frog that it was all right for him to relax and be himself, to which Sellers replied, "I could never be myself. You see, there is no me. I do not exist." *Time* pointed out that this was, in fact, more than mere humor. "The real Peter Sellers, at 54, is virtually a cipher," said the writer, and then quoted a lifelong friend of Sellers, who said, "Peter is the accumulation of all the roles he's played and all the people he's met. He's directing traffic inside all that." Sellers died six months later, presumably never knowing who he was.

Perhaps you think that the text in Acts 23:9 is speaking about you. *We find nothing wrong with this man.* We think there is nothing wrong with us. Actually, the text is an evaluation of the Apostle Paul after he had appeared before the Sanhedrin. Some of the Pharisees stood up and said that they could find nothing wrong with him. While Paul was glad to have their endorsement, he would have been the first person to differ theologically with this evaluation. While he had not transgressed any of their laws, he knew that there was something basically wrong with him and with the whole Sanhedrin and with us. In Romans 3:23 he said, "Since all have sinned and fall short of the glory of God; they are now justified by his grace as a gift, through the redemption that is in Christ Jesus."

The problem shared by everyone on this earth, and of everyone who has ever appeared on this earth, is that we are alienated from God. We are trying to live out our lives apart from God. We are trying to make it on our own. We are trying to make it on our wits and our skills and our looks and our family. Yet, we are not making it. What is wrong with us is that we are living life as if we did not need the Giver of life.

Jack Eckerd, the founder of Eckerd Drug Stores and an early benefactor of Eckerd College, has written a new book called *Eckerd: Finding the Right Prescription*. In it he tells of his spiritual growth and how Chuck Colson was instrumental in Eckerd's committing his life to Christ. He wrote:

> When Chuck and I were talking that day, about Watergate, he got a little irritated with my indecisiveness. "The problem with you, Jack," he said, "is that you won't decide whether to really buy into this thing. You keep sitting on the fence. You're supposed to be one of these hot-shot business guys who makes fast decisions; when are you going to make up your mind on the most important decision you'll ever make?" (*Eckerd*, p. 163)

Eckerd adds:

> Suddenly it was clear that Jesus took on my sins and the sins of others, and by doing this he purchased eternal life for us. My eternal life was not the result of what I had done for Him, but what Christ had done for me when He died on the cross. I realized that, at some point, I had to pray in faith and accept Christ's death for my sins, rather than trusting in my own deeds to make me God's child. . . . I made a decision to trust Him, and I have never been "on the fence," intellectually or emotionally, since that time. (*Eckerd*, pp. 163-64)

What about you? Are you on the fence, afraid to make a decision? The only thing that is wrong with you may be that you are denying yourself the most significant relationship of your life, a relationship with Jesus Christ. There is nothing wrong with you that Jesus, on the cross, has not repaired.

I read that the railroads lobbied to repeal a law that required them to have a caboose on every train, saying that the 1914 safety act was a tradition they could no longer afford. With the size of railroad crews being trimmed, no one was riding the caboose any more. They just dragged behind the train. A spokesman for the Norfolk Southern line said, "It's just a matter of dragging the doggone things around."

We live our lives in cabooses. Many of us are dragging a load in life that we don't have to drag. Now is the time, and here is the place to unload all that is unnecessary in life and make a commitment that will lighten the load. Jesus invites us to his table. To accept his invitation is a commitment on our part. We will never be the same again. When we depart from here, we will be new creatures in Christ.

What's *wrong* with you? Nothing that God can't fix right now in this sacrament.

WORLD COMMUNION 1

> *Thou hast made us to drink the wine of aston-ishment. (Ps. 60:3 KJV)*

Wine of Astonishment

Ho-hum, another World Communion Sunday. We have one every year on the first Sunday of October. Here we go again. It will be just like the last one and probably just like the next one. Nothing very exciting ever happens around the church. The crowds at the church are not exactly like the crowds at a football game, you know. Now there's a crowd!

I've been to one Monday night professional football game. I went with a person who drove some of the members of the little band that used to play behind the goal posts in the end zone. So we drove right onto the field and spent the whole time down there.

When you have been down on the field of a stadium, your ears literally ring when you leave, because the noise is deafening. The anticipation before the game is contagious. You just know something important is about to happen. The cheerleaders dance, the band plays, the crowd swells, the teams make an appearance, and the stands explode with noise! Clapping, screaming, yelling, horns, all kinds of noise makers, celebration, bragging, back slapping. Something super is about to happen! During the whole game, except for one quiet moment during the prayer, the whole stadium is in a perpetual state of commotion and expectation.

Though some Christian gatherings can manage it, I wouldn't want church to be as rowdy as a football game. I would not like to see the congregation clap at what goes on in church, because this is not a performance for you. It is an offering from all of us to God. It is worship of God. In any case, if I encouraged you to clap, you might get the idea that then you could also boo if you didn't like the sermon.

I would like to see you have the anticipation that something exciting is about to happen every time you enter the sanctuary. I appreciate the joy and celebration and camaraderie that are evident at most sporting events, the fanatical loyalty to a cause that some persons have.

The point of sports is for one team to win, but do you know that this is also an accurate description of what happened on Golgotha? Jesus' win was unbelievably astonishing to his followers! His victory over death was simply amazing! It was, as the Bible says, simply "too good to be true." It took them by surprise. It took their breath away. It was a win of astonishment.

"Ho-hum, Holy Communion."

We are in danger of not being astonished any more. We have heard it all before. Many of us were brought up on Jesus' victory over death, and it has been a part of our vocabulary for many years. We have tamed a wild and wonderful event. We have domesticated a Holy Spirit, who, by definition, was "born free." We have yawned at the cross, lounged on the altar, and fallen asleep in the middle of the game. Ho-hum, Holy Communion.

The psalmist in our text had undergone a number of emotional calamities. A shattering national defeat shook him out of his humdrum existence, and now he was beginning to see God's activity in what was happening to him and to his people. God was "in this place," and the psalmist was beginning to know it, and knowing it he was surprised:

Thou hast cast us off, thou hast scattered us, thou hast been displeased; O turn thyself to us again. Thou hast made the earth to tremble; thou hast broken it: heal the breaches thereof; for it shaketh. Thou hast shewed thy people hard things: thou hast made us to drink the wine of astonishment. (Ps. 60:1-3 KJV)

The psalmist is saying to God: "You are an amazing Person. You are an unpredictable Being. You cannot be bought or taught or tamed. You go where you want to go and do what you want to do, and I've never seen anything like that before on earth. You really surprise me."

> Amazing grace! How sweet the sound
> That saved a wretch like me!
> I once was lost, but now am found;
> Was blind, but now I see.

The Gospel of Mark reminds us of the reaction that Jesus continually got from his listeners. Were they bored when he spoke? Did they doodle on the bulletin cover when he preached? Did their minds wander as they thought about picnicking by the Sea of Galilee? Did they sit there thinking about the sleek camel they would ride across the desert when Jesus got through? Did they whisper under their breath, "Hohum, Jesus"?

Mark tells us of their reaction. They were astonished at his teaching! They were "amazed, and they kept on asking one another, 'What is this? A new teaching—with authority! He commands even the unclean spirits, and they obey him ' At once his fame began to spread throughout the surrounding region of Galilee" (Mark 1:27-28). Not only were they astonished by his teachings, but also they were astonished when he willingly died and proclaimed that his death meant that all human beings were forgiven for their sins, and now any barrier that had previously been erected between them and God was overcome. That is amazing grace. Lloyd John Ogilvie wrote, "I have come to believe that an outward evidence of the indwelling of the Holy Spirit is the capacity to be constantly astonished at what God is up to in our lives. A bored, bland, unsurprisable Christian is a contradiction of terms" (Lloyd John Ogilivie, *The Cup of Wonder* [Grand Rapids, Mich.: Baker Book House, 1985], p. 139).

In a moment we shall join with millions of Christians around the world as we commune at this table that extends today to every corner of the universe. Now, as you partake of the wine of astonishment, sip the new wine of love, drink the new wine of forgiveness, gulp the new wine of peace, swallow the new wine of amazing grace, empty the cup of wonder, and experience the last drops of the new wine of final victory.

If there is a stranger here, maybe someone who has never participated in the celebration of the sacrament of Holy Communion before, would that person explain our joy by saying that we are filled with this new wine? The win of astonishment has produced this wine of astonishment.

WORLD COMMUNION 2

> *There is no longer Jew or Greek, there is no longer slave or free, there is no longer male and female; for all of you are one in Christ Jesus.*
> *(Gal. 3:28)*

Loosening Your Belt

I t is estimated that in the year 2000 there will be more Christians in Africa than in the whole of North America, and more Christians in Latin America than in Europe. It is a fact that over six million new converts have been added to the Christian community every year on the continent of Africa in recent decades.

What this means is that in sheer numbers the axis of the Christian faith is shifting from Europe and North America to the Third World, which is sometimes called the "Two-thirds World."

In Christ there is no east or west. On World Communion Sunday, we are reminded that all humankind is present at the same table as guests of Christ. Today, we think of Christians in Nepal and Pakistan and Thailand and throughout the world, coming to this table of our Lord. This is his table, the Lord's table.

Robert Shelton wrote in *Reformed Liturgy and Music,* "This sacrament proclaims that as Christians already we are one, no matter how much we want it otherwise and keep insisting on it otherwise, for Christ cannot be divided. Christ is one" (Robert Shelton, "What's in a Name?" *Reformed Liturgy and Music,* 19 [Winter 1985]: 14-17). On World Communion Sunday we proclaim that we are one in Christ Jesus, "all distinctions have vanished" (Gal. 3:28 Twentieth Century New Testament).

> *"Anything that would deny our oneness in Christ . . . is a sin."*

Robert L. Wilson and William H. Willimon have published a twenty-one page study called "The Seven Churches of Methodism." Most of us are familiar with the fact that racism is a sin, that sexism is a sin, and that ageism is a sin. To discriminate against anyone because of color, sex, or age is not only illegal in America, but also it is and has been a sin everywhere, for God loves us all equally and cares for us all equally and wants the best for us all equally. The study has concluded that there is another "ism" to add to that list of sins: regionalism. "Regional differences may be a far greater source of unrest in The United Methodist Church than any other factor." They detail how United Methodism is divided up into the Industrial Northeast, the Church South, the Midwest, and so forth. Each region has its own distinctive theology and way of worshiping and thinking. The authors claim that "although some conflicts in The United Methodist Church appear on the surface to be over ideology, polity, or between racial and cultural differences, the underlying causes may be regional differences."

Regionalism may be the most predominant sin of the 1990s. Anything that would deny our oneness in Christ, our oneness as human beings with one another, is a sin. Christ wants us to be one according to his prayer to the Father in John 17, when he prayed that "they may be one, as we are one" (John 17:11).

All distinctions have vanished. Do you find that hard to believe? Remember when Colonel Duke landed on the moon and drove the lunar rover around as a member of the Apollo 16 crew? As he settled down to do the assigned experiments, he looked up at the earth and stood silent for a moment, taking in the wonder of where he was.

He said that at first it seemed incongruous to look up at the earth. After all, we are accustomed to looking up at the moon and down at the earth. For some inexplicable reason, he lifted his open hand upward toward the earth, and suddenly realized that the palm of his hand could completely block from view the whole world.

Then he said that for the first time in his life, he began to understand the oneness, the wholeness, the singleness of the world. From that moment on, his perception of the world as one community has been strengthened.

The study of The United Methodist Church, mentioned above, reminds us that regionalism still exists in our world and in our church, but Christ has come to forgive sin and to give us the power to resist temptation. One of those temptations is to think regionally. Some people say that they are from the Bible belt or the industrial belt or the corn belt or the sun belt. We know of two huge walls that serve as symbols of humankind's desire to separate themselves from one another: the Great Wall of China and the Berlin Wall. But now the sun has set on these walls. The Son of God eliminates all regional thinking, whatever "belt" it be.

Many years ago, Rudyard Kipling wrote in "The Ballad of East and West": "Oh, East is East, and West is West, and never the twain shall meet." Well, I am here to tell you that there is One who is greater than rigid racial, social, and regional barriers. And that One is Christ the Lord, who now declares on World Communion Sunday that all these human barriers have vanished, for in union with Christ you are all one.

> In Christ there is no east or west,
> In him no south or north;
> But one great fellowship of love
> Throughout the whole wide earth.

Let us now join the Lord and all his people everywhere at his table.

ORDINARY COMMUNION 1

> *I am the light of the world. Whoever follows me
> will never walk in darkness but will have the
> light of life. (John 8:12)*

*Pentecost and
Polaroids*

Happy birthday! Happy birthday to every Christian church in the world. Today is called the birthday of the Christian church because we celebrate Pentecost on this seventh Sunday after Jesus' resurrection. The word *pentecost* means fifty, and approximately fifty days after Easter, Acts 2 tells us, the disciples gathered to celebrate the Jewish Pentecost (Feast of Weeks) and to observe the consecration of the harvest season. On this day, "from heaven there came a sound like the rush of a violent wind, and it filled the entire house where they were sitting. Divided tongues, as of fire, appeared among them, and a tongue rested on each one of them. All of them were filled with the Holy Spirit" (Acts 2:2-4). The promised arrival of the Spirit of God had finally come. From this point on, the disciples began to preach with renewed vigor and commitment, and the Christian church began to grow.

The prophet Joel had said, "Then afterward I will pour out my spirit on all flesh" (Joel 2:28). Jesus said that when he left us he would send us a Comforter, the Holy Spirit, to be with us. That day of promise had arrived. The Holy Spirit was giving birth to a new thing, and the Christian church was christened by fire and enthusiasm. In a real sense, on Pentecost the disciples were affirmed in their ministry and commissioned to their work.

Having just finished another family wedding, we must have forty of those Polaroid pictures lying around the house. I really don't know how a Polaroid camera works. You put in the film, snap the picture, and wait. At first, you think that nothing has happened. The film is gray, and there is no picture at all. But as the light exposes the film, slowly an image appears. At first the picture is hazy and colorless. As the seconds tick by, the picture you took becomes clear. You keep looking, and finally you see what was there in the first place.

> *"An image began to form, which is the truest image there ever was."*

Something like that experience happened to the early disciples after Pentecost. Slowly, over a period of time, as they received the power of the Holy Spirit, they learned who Jesus was. They began to see clearly for themselves. It did not happen all at once, but as they exposed themselves to the Light, slowly an image began to form, which is the truest image there ever was.

Jesus said: "I am the light of the world. Whoever follows me will never walk in darkness but will have the light of life" (John 8:12). As this image of Jesus developed in the minds of the members of the early church, they grew in boldness and in faith. As they felt the presence of the Holy Spirit guiding them each day, they focused on the purpose of their lives. Pentecost produced for them a perfect picture of who they were and what they should be doing in this world.

Jerold Lucy, an editor of a medical journal, feels that there is a movement in the medical field today toward more gentleness in the care of patients. He reported how the Presbyterian

Hospital in New York has reduced the use of tracheal tubes and ventilators with infants whenever possible. The hospital staff discovered that the use of warm, moist air, blown into the nostrils, seems to bring greater success than the former method. The hospital has had better success keeping infants alive, allowing them to breathe freely, and reports fewer cases of chronic lung disease with this new gentler method.

> ## *"We don't need any more power brokers."*

This report is a reminder that the gentle touch is most often the one thing needed in life. We don't need any more power brokers. We don't need any more pushing and shoving. We don't need any more loud mouths screaming in our ears. We don't need any more high pressure television salespersons/evangelists reaching for our wallets. Our world needs the softer, quieter touch. In order to breathe freely, we need a more gentle ministry from Christ's church. In order to be healed and whole, we need gentle love.

A little girl was walking home with her mother one Sunday after the church service. "You know, Mommy," said the little girl, "I heard the minister say God is bigger than we are. Well, if God is bigger than we are, and if he is inside of us, won't he show through? Won't everybody see him?"

"Yes, dear," her mother answered, "if God lives in us we can't hide him there. Everyone will see him."

I live close to the lighthouse at Hillsboro Inlet, and so I appreciate the fact that on the Eddystone Lighthouse on the coast of England, these words are inscribed: "To give light is to save a life." Every time I see our lighthouse now, I will think of that inscription: "To give light is to save a life."

Jesus, as he died on the cross, claimed to be this dark world's Light. This sacrament lights all the dark corners of our lives as Jesus gave to save a life.

ORDINARY COMMUNION 2

If you then, who are evil, know how to give good gifts to your children, how much more will your Father in heaven give good things to those who ask him! (Matt. 7:11)

God Gives Strength

Manuel Garcia has stomach cancer. He is thirty-nine years old and lives in Milwaukee, Wisconsin. He has been undergoing chemotherapy and now has lost all of his hair. His older brother, Julio, his close relatives, and many friends all felt emotionally handcuffed by their inability to help him or do anything for him. What could they do to let him know they cared for him, to let him know that they would do anything for him to make his situation more bearable?

Finally, the relatives decided that they would visit Manuel at the Milwaukee County Medical Complex, but before they went they all shaved their heads. Now they all were like Manuel. They were going to show him that bald is beautiful. His friends and family were going to stand with him in his time of need.

The following day, Manual was discharged from the hospital and returned home to discover that over one hundred neighborhood friends had also shaved their heads as a symbol that they were going to identify with him in a difficult time. Garcia said, "If a lot of people did for other cancer patients what my friends are doing for me, it would help" (*People Weekly,* August 26, 1985, p. 51).

Your existence upon the earth, the existence of each one of us, is terminal. Some of us may have fifty or sixty more years left, but few of us will be alive eighty years from now. How are we going to face that fact? Well, it turns out that we have a friend who doesn't want us to face it alone. "If you then, who are evil, know how to give good gifts to your children, how much more will your Father in heaven give good things to those who ask him!" (Matt. 7:11). God wanted to give us a good gift. Our Father in heaven has decided to identify closely with us, just as Manuel Garcia's friends identified closely with him. God decided to enter our world as one of us. While he didn't shave his head, he did identify closely with us.

> *"We still must die, but the sting has been removed."*

God was so concerned about us that he became one of us and went through death for us so that the sting of death might be removed. We still must die, but the sting has been removed. Through faith in God we now know that upon death we will enter a more meaningful life with God through Jesus Christ.

God, in Christ, has shown his deep commitment to us. God, in Christ, has shown his great love for us. On the cross Jesus expressed God's desire to redirect our lives so that we might spend our short time here on earth serving him and glorifying him with all that he has given us. The sacrament of Holy Communion is a celebration of the fact that God wants to give his people strength in times of weakness, hope in times of despair, love in times of hate, and peace in times of turmoil. God wants to shower upon us many blessings. We don't have a God who stands over against us, but One who stands with us. He is on our side to empower us. This is what is made available in this holy sacrament—strength, hope, love, and peace.

Several years ago a school teacher assigned to visit children in a large city hospital received a routine call requesting that she visit a particular child. She took the boy's name and room number and was told by the teacher on the other end of the line, "We're studying nouns and adverbs in his class now. I'd be grateful if you could help him with his homework, so he doesn't fall behind the others."

It wasn't until the visiting teacher got outside the boy's room that she realized it was located in the hospital's burn unit. No one had prepared her to find a young boy horribly burned and in great pain. She felt that she couldn't just turn around and walk out, so she awkwardly stammered, "I'm the hospital teacher, and your teacher sent me to help you with nouns and adverbs."

The boy was in such pain that he barely responded. She stumbled through his English lesson, ashamed at putting him through such a senseless exercise. The next morning, a nurse on the burn unit asked her, "What did you do to that boy?" Before she could finished a profusion of apologies, the nurse interrupted her, "You don't understand. We've been very worried about him, but ever since you were here yesterday, his whole attitude has changed. He's fighting back, responding to treatment. It's as though he's decided to live."

The boy later explained that he had completely given up hope until he saw that teacher. It all changed when he came to a simple realization. With joyful tears, he expressed it this way, "They wouldn't send a teacher to work on nouns and adverbs with a dying boy, would they?"

God has come in this sacrament to work with us on our weaknesses. He wants to give us strength. He has come to work on our despair; he wants to give us hope. He has come to work on the hatred that we have between each other; he wants to give us love. He has come to work on the turmoil in our lives; he wants to give us peace. God wouldn't send a Teacher to work with us on these things if we were dying, would he?

ORDINARY COMMUNION 3

> *So neither the one who plants nor the one who waters is anything, but only God who gives the growth. (I Cor. 3:7)*

Fellow Gardeners

On this holy occasion, the Apostle Paul might begin by saying, "I'd like to recognize the presence of the revered clergy, the esteemed elders, the director of music, the organist, and the outstanding choir. I would like to acknowledge among us the many friends and visitors. I would like to recognize all the honored members of the congregation this morning and all other gardeners."

Yes, I said "gardeners," because Paul, in our text, makes it clear that we are all working in the same field. We all have the same status in the service of the Lord. We are gardeners, working in the field for the same Master. All of us have the same footing. All of us have been charged with the same responsibilities. All of us are equally called to our duties. Paul is especially eager that each one of us realizes that we are all called to be servants of the one Master. He wrote to another church: "I say to everyone among you not to think of yourself more highly than you ought to think" (Rom. 12:3). It was important to him that all Christians know who they are.

The Apostle Paul established the church in Corinth, and it had gotten off to a good start, but somewhere along the way jealousy and strife began to appear. Churches, you know, have personalities just as individual people do. Some churches are loving and kind. Some are boisterous and loud. Some are passive and quiet. Some are servants. Some behave like royalty.

Some are bellicose. The Corinthian church was developing into a cantankerous, bickering, suspicious group of people who were undermining the leadership of that church. Some were defending Paul as if he were the real leader of the church. Some were defending Apollos against Paul, as if he were the real leader of the church. Few seemed to be defending Jesus Christ as the head and leader of the church. I can just hear the Corinthians saying, "Jesus who?" They were intent on fighting. They were "babes in Christ" whose most prominent characteristics, according to the Bible, were envy, strife, and an ability to separate themselves into hostile divisions.

Paul's first letter to them was an attempt to call them back to their origins. They must return to their religious roots. They must get rid of their pride and their feelings of self-importance. They needed to know that Paul was nothing, Apollos was nothing, and, therefore, they were nothing—nothing but gardeners working in the field of the Lord, some planting, some watering, some hoeing, some weeding, some pruning, some cultivating—all gardeners for the Owner. No one should think of himself or herself more highly than he or she ought to think, for we are all humble laborers together. Some plant, some water, but God gives the increase.

John Witherspoon was the only clergyman to sign the Declaration of Independence. He was president of what we now call Princeton University, a man highly regarded in the early history of the nation and the church. He was asked to preach at the first meeting of the General Assembly of the Presbyterian Church on May 21, 1789, and to be acting moderator until a permanent one was elected later in the meeting. He performed this task admirably as one of the most visible and highly respected people of his day, even though he had lost his health, the vision in one of his eyes, and he would die within five years of signing the Declaration.

> *"We are called into Christ's body not to argue, criticize, or complain but to humbly serve."*

On this occasion, Witherspoon chose to use I Corinthians 3:7, a text that he also used when he was installed as the pastor of the Presbyterian Church of Princeton, New Jersey, so we know it was a favorite. He wanted the early Presbyterians to know that if they were going to succeed in America they would have to view themselves as simple gardeners in God's field, tillers of God's earth. They would have to perform faithfully their humble duties in lowly fashion, be faithful to those duties, and let the increase be in God's hands.

Today the church of Jesus Christ needs to remember this message of John Witherspoon and the Apostle Paul. We are today the body of Jesus Christ on earth, and Jesus Christ was a humble servant. He must be our model. We are called into Christ's body not to argue, criticize, or complain but to humbly serve. Someone has said, "If you want to fight, join the Marines. If you want to love, join the church."

Bonnie Russell has written a simple poem called "Love Loves":

> Love is nothing until it loves.
> Love is nothing until it shares. . . .

Jesus said, "No one has greater love than this, to lay down one's life for one's friends" (John 15:13). Friend, this is what Jesus has done for you and what we and millions of others celebrate in the Lord's Supper. This celebration shows Jesus' great love for us.

ORDINARY COMMUNION 4

> *This is my body that is for you. Do this in*
> *remembrance of me. (I Cor. 11:24)*

Be My Guest

The table spread before you is not my table. The table spread before you is not a denominational table, or a First Church table. This table is not the church officers' table, even though they have prepared it for us. It is not a deacons' table, even though they will clean up after us. This is the Lord's table, and the celebration that we are about to observe is the Lord's Supper. What we are about to do belongs to our Lord.

God is the host at this supper. God is the One who has made all of this possible. God is the One who has issued the invitations. God is the One who desires our presence here. You may have read about this observance in the bulletin, but it was God who issued the invitations. Because God is the host at this supper, it is obvious that we are the guests. God says to us, "Be my guest," and we have responded by coming here to receive this sacrament. It would be rude if the host invited us and then did not show up. God has promised to be spiritually present in this bread and wine. We are present in our bodies, and soon our bodies will partake of the spiritual presence of Almighty God.

The invitation that I will soon give from behind the Lord's table is this: "All that humbly put their trust in Christ, and desire His help that they may lead a holy life, all that are truly sorry for their sins and would be delivered from the burden of them, are invited and encouraged in His name to come to this

Sacrament. Let us, therefore, so come that we may find refreshing and rest unto our souls" (*The Book of Common Worship* [Philadelphia: The Board of Christian Education of the Presbyterian Church, 1946], p. 169).

> *"A lack of baptism is the only basis for exclusion from this supper."*

Our Protestant liturgy makes it clear that the invitation to the Lord's Supper is extended to all who have been baptized. Theologically speaking, a lack of baptism is the only basis for exclusion from this supper. All baptized Christians are invited and encouraged to come to this meal. It is a supper for baptized members of Christ's church. Note that you do not even have to be a confirmed member of the church to partake. You do not have to be thirteen or in the seventh grade to participate. There is no age discrimination at either end—either too young or too old. This supper is for the spiritual nourishment of all who have taken their faith seriously enough that they have been baptized. All who have received the sacrament of baptism are invited to receive the sacrament of Holy Communion. No one is excluded. This is an open communion. Humankind has divided up the body of Christ, but at the table of our Lord we are all one again. Isn't that exciting? As Paul wrote to the church in Corinth, "Because there is one bread, we who are many are one body, for we all partake of the one bread" (I Cor. 10:17).

We all come, not because we are worthy, but because we must. We come because it is a privilege given to the undeserving who come in faith, repentance, and love. Even if you doubt the efficacy of this sacrament, even if your trust is faulty, you are encouraged to come to have that doubt removed and that trust strengthened. This, then, is an evangelistic meal that is reaching out to all who believe fully, and also to those who only half believe. "I believe; help my unbelief!" said the father of the sick child when Jesus asked him to believe (Mark 9:24 REB). He was saying, "I have faith, help me where faith falls short." This meal is not just for those full of faith. It is also for the half-full. It is for all of us when faith falls short.

"Come! Come," says the Lord. "Come to be assured of God's love and grace in Christ Jesus. Come, be my guest."

Extraordinary Sermon Illustrations

There has been so much emphasis on the feelings of the giver that we have often ignored the fact that the gift is also a very important part of the giver. We will give what we feel, and hence the gift is related to the feelings of the giver. "It's not the gift, but the thought behind it that matters," we have so often said, but that is a half-truth. The gift also matters. It, too, must be appropriate for the occasion and for the person to whom you give it.

We would not give the pastor a six-pack of beer, even though we were very sincere and really wanted the pastor to be merry. We would not sincerely give a teenager a carton of cigarettes for Christmas, or a young child a box of razor blades. It is important that we have the right motive when we give, but it is also important that we give the right gift. You may love your child more than anyone else in the world, but you would be wrong to give him or her a bottle of aspirin to chew on like Christmas candy.

* * *

There is the story of a minister's daughter who one evening interrupted her father's reading of the newspaper with the statement, "Daddy, we have a play for you." He writes:

> Obediently I followed her into the living room. Right away I knew it was a Christmas play for at the foot of the piano stool was a lighted flashlight wrapped in swaddling clothes lying in a shoe box.

Rex (age six) came in wearing my bathrobe and carrying a mop handle. He sat on the stool, and looked at the flashlight. Nancy draped a sheet over her head and stood behind Rex.

"I'm Mary and this is Joseph," she said. Enter Trudy, with a pillowcase over her arms, saying, "I'm an angel." Then came Anne; I knew she was a wise man because she moved as if she were riding a camel. On a pillow she carried three items, undoubtedly gold, frankincense, and myrrh.

Anne then bowed to the flashlight, to Mary, to Joseph, to Trudy, to me, then announced, "I'm all three wise men. I bring precious gifts: gold, circumstance and mud!"

Naturally the father did his best to suppress a laugh, but you know it does make sense to bring to Christ our gold, circumstance, and mud.

1. *Our gold,* which entombs us, and that we think makes life go around. Our money, which we strive to get and lose so quickly at death. What better gift to bring to God than a gift of money? It is the symbol of all we hold dear at Christmas and at all times, a symbol of our commitment to him.

2. *Our circumstance.* Every one of us is in a particular circumstance. We are surrounded by certain problems that continually bother us. We worry about our own health or the health of a friend; we worry about our children's education or the work that we do; we are tempted on every hand. What a practical gift to bring God this year—the circumstance in which we find ourselves. No matter what it is, how worthy it is, or how humiliating it is, bring it to God, turn it over to God, and let God have it.

3. *Our mud.* Mud is, of course, made out of clean water with a lot of dirt added. This is the story of our lives, isn't it? So many of us have muddied up our lives little by little with many grains of dirt until our lives are not just dirty water, but are mud, and we are stuck in it.

What better gifts could we bring to God this Christmas than our gold, our circumstance, and our mud? When we give God this present, when we present him with the gift of our lives, he will turn our gold into his glory, our circumstance into a stance for him, and our mud into a pool of forgiveness.

All God wants for Christmas is you—gold, circumstance, and mud—the most appropriate gift.

* * *

Years ago in an express agency in Shanghai, China, there was a sign printed in English that delighted tourists because of its inadvertent humor. It read: "Your baggage taken and delivered in all directions." Unfortunately, our imagination does not have to be stretched much to apply that sign to our times, for who would deny that one of the signs of the times is that most of us are being delivered in all directions simultaneously?

Only recently does the gobbledygook that was contained in a directive from the British Admiralty begin to make sense to me, and I worry that it does make sense to me, but I contribute it to the tenor of our times. That directive was, "It is necessary for technical reasons that these warheads should be stored upside down, that is with the top at the bottom and the bottom at the top. In order that there may be no doubt as to which is the bottom and which is the top, for storage purposes, it will be seen that the bottom of each warhead has been labeled with the word, 'TOP.'"

Scripture shows us that early Christians were not being pulled in all directions, for they had a common purpose: "The whole group of those who believed were of one heart and soul" (Acts 4:32). They were united around a common goal. They knew what their reason for living was and why they were there.

* * *

Oscar Wilde said, "Jesus was a lover for whom the world was too small." Our problem is that our love hardly goes beyond ourselves and our families. Let us realize as we partake of World Communion that we are bound together with fellow Christians around the world in a common purpose, a common life, a common conviction, and a common concern for others. "All one body we."

* * *

A Spartan king once boasted to a visiting monarch about the walls of Sparta. The visiting monarch looked around but could see no walls. He said to the Spartan king, "Where are these walls about which you speak and boast so much?" The Spartan king pointed to his citizens and said, "There are the walls of Sparta, and every one of them a brick."

So long as a brick lies by itself it is useless. It becomes of use only when it is built into a building. This is why it was made! And only when it is built into a building does it realize its function and the reason for its existence. It is so with each individual Christian. To realize our destiny, we must not remain alone, but must be built into the fabric and edifice of the church. Just as Christ is the cornerstone of the church, so also must we be joined with him in that living building.

* * *

In a small college town, a tavern frequented by students ran the following ad in the campus paper during the days before Parents' Weekend: "Bring Your Parents for Lunch Saturday. We'll Pretend We Don't Know You."

The ad was soon challenged by the college chaplain, who posted a revised version on the campus bulletin board. It read: "Bring Your Parents to Chapel Sunday. We'll Pretend We Know You Well."

* * *

Christianity makes strange "breadfellows." Now I didn't say "bedfellows"; I said "breadfellows." The word *companion* is from two Latin words, *com* (which means "with") and *panis* (which means "bread"). The word *companion* literally means "with bread," or, as the dictionary says, a "breadfellow." Today we are "breadfellows" with the whole world, for on World Communion Sunday the whole world is our companion.

* * *

A former president of Duke University, President Few, was on his way to church one Sunday morning in the rain when some students recognized him and offered him a ride. He accepted, and on the way they asked him why he had decided to go to church that morning on such a rainy day.

President Few said, "I didn't decide this morning. I decided fifty-five years ago, and I haven't had to ask myself that question since." For him it was a settled issue. He didn't have to decide every Sunday morning whether he was going to go. It was settled a long time ago when he gave his life to Jesus Christ. He had decided then that he would be with Jesus' people in God's house, learning about God's will for his life every Sunday. No matter where he traveled, he knew where he would be on Sunday morning: in some church worshiping God.

* * *

The late author/preacher Lloyd C. Douglas told how he once asked an old music teacher, "Well, what's the good news today?" The old man went over to a tuning fork suspended by a cord, struck it with a mallet, and said, "That, my friend, is A. It was A all day yesterday. It will be A all day tomorrow, next week, and for a thousand years. The soprano upstairs warbles off key, the tenor next door flats on his high ones, and the piano across the hall is out of tune. But that," he said, striking the tuning fork again, "is A. And that, my friend, is the good news for today."

Some things never change. The navigator needs the North Star, the designer and the builder need the plumb line, the scientist needs the square root, and the musician needs the fixed note.

Jesus Christ is the fixed point for all Christians. By him we tune our lives. In him we find our example.

* * *

Faith must not be a form of escapism, unrealistic and irrelevant. A news item that appeared in a Canadian paper during the hunting season: "Sam Higgins was accidentally shot yesterday while hunting. One of the wounds was pronounced fatal, but his friends will be glad to hear that the other wounds are not considered dangerous." Surely the reality of an event was never more sweetly sugar-coated.

* * *

In the 1950s, when television began its influence over our minds, a classic television advertisement had to do with encyclopedias. A child, looking up into his father's eyes, asked, "Daddy, why is the sky blue?" Of course, the father didn't have the faintest idea why the sky is blue. But he simply turned in his swivel chair, opened an encyclopedia on the shelf behind him, and discovered the answer. This was supposed to be a subtle hint to daddies all over America that if they don't want to look stupid in front of their children, they had better purchase this encyclopedia fast. That's the way it was in the 1950s.

But in the 1990s the scenario has changed. The questions are a little tougher, and the children are a great deal more sophisticated. The child now asks, "Daddy, why are there so many wars? Why does the Ku Klux Klan hate blacks? Why did Iraq invade Kuwait? Why are some people in the public trust and privilege dishonest and greedy? Why can't I freely travel anywhere in the world? Why are there so many barriers?"

The Christian faith has been established to break these barriers. The Christian faith proclaims that all are equal in the sight of God, that God loves all of us with an undying love, and that if we do not love other people, we cannot love God.

* * *

A pastor in Maine tells about the game between the first-place and last-place teams in a YMCA basketball league for junior high boys. In YMCA basketball, there is a rule that everyone on each team must get a chance to play. So at the start of the fourth quarter, both coaches began to substitute freely. On the losing team's bench there was a boy who hadn't gotten to play much all year. With four minutes left to play, the coach sent this boy in.

It was obvious after two or three times up and down the court that this boy wasn't like the other boys. He was slower, not just physically but mentally, too. While the teams were racing one way for the basket, he was often racing the other way. Oh, he'd turn around, but by then they'd be heading the other way again. Finally, there came a time when both the boy and the teams were heading in the same direction, and by mistake somebody threw the ball to him. Everything stopped. The officials froze. The crowd hushed. All the players stopped where they were. And this great defensive team, the number-one team in the league, the pride of their coach for not allowing more than thirty points a game, stood still and dropped their hands to their sides.

The boy turned the ball in his hands a couple times, looked at the basket, took two or three steps without dribbling the ball, and shot. He missed. But someone caught the ball and passed it back to him. Still no one moved. He turned the ball in his hands again, looked at the basket, took two or three more steps without dribbling, and shot. The ball hit the rim and bounced in.

A roar went up, and the boy jumped up and down with glee. There wasn't a dry eye in the gymnasium. The clock stopped, another player came in, and the boy went back to the bench. The game went on until the final buzzer, but during that game a barrier had been broken. A boy who had been the butt of many jokes and cruel tricks all year had been accepted and encouraged.

* * *

A company that employed several thousand people was attempting to institute a new pension plan, but the plan could not be implemented unless there was 100 percent participation by all the employees. Every employee signed up except for one, who absolutely refused to budge. His fellow workers talked to him, his union steward talked to him, his foreman talked to him, but every effort to win him over failed. It seemed as if the company would not be able to buy the new pension for the employees. Finally, the president of the company called the man into his office and said, "Here is a copy of the proposed plan, and here is a pen. Sign your name, or you are fired." The man quickly picked up the pen and signed. Then the president said, "I don't understand why you have refused to sign until now." The employee responded, "Well, sir, until now no one had taken the time to explain the policy quite so clearly to me as you just did."

The celebration of the sacrament of Holy Communion is not new to most of us. We have been here before, but I'm hoping it might be explained more clearly to you than ever before.

* * *

When a newscaster was interviewing people on the street just before the election of Pope John II, he asked a fourteen-year-old girl, "What would you like to do if you were the pope?" Her reply was, "I'd cover the Communion wafers with chocolate."

* * *

During World War II in France, some soldiers with their sergeant brought the body of a dead comrade to a cemetery to have their friend buried there. The priest told them gently that it was a Roman Catholic cemetery, and he was bound to ask whether their comrade had been a baptized adherent of the Roman Catholic Church.

They said they did not know. The priest said that he was very sorry, but, if that was the case, he could not permit burial in his churchyard. So the soldiers took their comrade away and sadly buried him just outside the fence of the churchyard.

The next day, they came back to see if the grave was all right, and to their astonishment they could not find it. They knew that it was only six feet from the fence of the cemetery, but search as they might they could find no trace of the freshly dug soil. As they were about to leave in bewilderment, the priest came up to them. He told them that his heart had been troubled because of his refusal to allow their dead comrade to be buried in the churchyard, so early that morning he had risen from his bed and, with his own hands, had moved the fence to include the body of the soldier who had died for France.

* * *

One of the most sacred objects to the early Native Americans was their peace pipe, or calumet as it is called. The peace pipe was used to bring reconciliation between hostile people. In the heat of battle, if an adversary were to offer the peace pipe to his opponent, and the opponent accepted it, the weapons on both sides were at once laid down. The peace pipe became the symbol of peace. Today, in our battles we are also being offered peace, through Christ our Lord in this sacrament. We are about to "pass the peace." Will you make God your peace by becoming a personal peacemaker?

Suggested Reading

Barth, Marcus. *Rediscovering the Lord's Supper: Communion with Israel, with Christ, and Among the Guests.* Philadelphia: John Knox, 1988.

Beardslee, William A., et. al. *Biblical Preaching on the Death of Jesus.* Nashville: Abingdon Press, 1989.

Bridge, Donald, and David Phypers. *The Meal That Unites?* London: Hodder & Stoughton, 1981.

Daniels, Harold M. *What to Do with Sunday Morning.* Philadelphia: Westminster Press, 1979.

Heron, Alasdair. *Table and Tradition.* Philadelphia: Westminster Press, 1983.

Jenson, Robert W. *Visible Words: The Interpretation and Practice of Christian Sacraments.* Philadelphia: Fortress Press, 1978.

Kinnamon, Michael. *Why It Matters: A Popular Introduction to the Baptism, Eucharist, and Ministry Text.* Geneva: World Council of Churches, 1985.

Marty, Martin E. *The Lord's Supper.* Philadelphia: Fortress Press, 1980.

Reumann, John Henry Paul. *The Supper of the Lord: The New Testament, Ecumenical Dialogues, and Faith and Order on Eucharist.* Philadelphia: Fortress Press, 1985.

White, James E. *Sacraments as God's Self-Giving.* Nashville: Abingdon Press, 1983.

Willimon, William H. *Preaching and Leading Worship.* Philadelphia: Westminster Press, 1984.